This is Wimbledon
The official guide to The Championships

By Alan Little
Honorary Librarian
Wimbledon Lawn Tennis Museum

All England Lawn Tennis and Croquet Club
Wimbledon, London

2013

Contents

Thirty Third Edition 2013   ISBN 978 1 899039 41 8

Chairman's Welcome

I would like to extend a very warm welcome to Wimbledon for the 2013 Championships.

Whilst we have no new developments around the Grounds to highlight this year, we have made significant announcements about our future investment both in the sport and our facilities here at The All England Lawn Tennis Club.

Firstly, we have, after consultation with the relevant bodies, agreed a change to the established calendar from 2015 onwards, with The Championships starting a week later. This will allow for three weeks of grass court play between Roland Garros and Wimbledon and more time for players to adapt to the change of surface. So, some early warning for your 2015 diaries, with The Championships commencing on Monday 29th June.

Secondly, we have recently unveiled our Master Plan for the long-term development of the Grounds. The changes – which we hope will see the introduction of a roof on No. 1 Court by 2019 – will improve your Championships' experience, with improved facilities in many areas. We are very excited by the proposals, which will be delivered on a phased basis over the next decade or so.

As with previous years, play on Centre and No. 1 Courts is scheduled to start at 1.00pm each day (except the two Finals' days in the case of Centre Court, when play will commence at 2.00pm). Play on all other courts will, however, start at the slightly earlier time of 11.30am for at least the first eight days. The Gentlemen's and Ladies' Wheelchair competition will again be played during the last three days of the Championships.

As usual, we will have a number of security measures in place to offer you a safe and secure environment. Inevitably these arrangements will affect everyone coming into our Grounds, but I am certain that you will both understand why they exist and will bear with them.

Philip Brook

Philip Brook
Chairman, Committee of Management of
The Championships, Wimbledon

The History of Wimbledon

Introduction

The Lawn Tennis Championships at Wimbledon have developed from the garden party atmosphere of the first meeting in 1877, witnessed by a few hundred spectators, to a highly professional tournament attracting an attendance of nearly 500,000 people, and through the press, radio and television a following of millions throughout the world.

The Tournament starts each year six weeks before the first Monday in August and lasts for a fortnight or for as long as necessary to complete all events. Players from over 60 nations regularly compete.

Over 6,000 people are at the ground for the period of The Championships to do a job in connection with the Tournament. These include a temporary staff of several hundred who are directly employed by The All England Lawn Tennis Club and others who are provided by firms, contractors, voluntary bodies and public services, as well as representatives of the media.

In short, during the Fortnight at the end of June and the beginning of July the Club is a hive of activity, squarely in the eye of the sporting world.

The Beginning

The All England Lawn Tennis and Croquet Club, which is responsible for staging the world's leading tennis tournament, is a private Club founded in 1868 originally as 'The All England Croquet Club' and its first ground was situated off Worple Road, Wimbledon.

In 1875 lawn tennis, a game introduced by Major Walter Clopton Wingfield a year or so earlier and originally called "Sphairistike", was added to the activities of the Club. In the spring of 1877 the Club was re-titled 'The All England Croquet and Lawn Tennis Club' and signalled its change of name by instituting the first Lawn Tennis Championship. A new code of laws, hitherto administered by the M.C.C., was drawn up for the meeting. These have stood the test of time and today's rules are similar except for details such as the height of the net and posts and the distance of the service line from the net.

The only event held in 1877 was the Gentlemen's Singles which was won by Spencer Gore, an old Harrovian rackets player, from a field of 22. About 200 spectators paid one shilling to watch the final.

The lawns at the ground were arranged in such a way that the principal court was situated in the middle with the others arranged around it; hence the title "Centre Court", which was retained when the Club moved in 1922 to the present site in Church Road, although not a true description of its location. However, in 1980 four new courts were brought into commission on the north side of the ground, which meant that the Centre Court was once more correctly defined. The opening of the new No. 1 Court in 1997 emphasised the description.

By 1882 activity at the Club was almost exclusively confined to lawn tennis and that year the word "croquet" was dropped from the title. However, for sentimental reasons, it was restored in 1899 and since then the title has remained "The All England Lawn Tennis and Croquet Club".

Enter the Ladies

In 1884 the Ladies' Singles was inaugurated and from an entry of 13 players Maud Watson became champion. That same year the Gentlemen's Doubles was started, the trophy being donated to the Club by Oxford University L.T.C. on cessation of their doubles championship, played from 1879 to 1883.

As the popularity of Wimbledon increased the facilities for the spectators were suitably improved. Permanent stands gradually took the place of temporary accommodation as by the mid-eighties crowds flocked to see the prowess of the Renshaw twins, Ernest and William. The boom became known as the "Renshaw-rush".

For a period in the nineties public affection for Wimbledon waned, but in 1897 the legendary Doherty brothers, Laurie and Reggie, began their ten year rule of the courts and soon capacity crowds reappeared.

Overseas Champions

By the turn of the century Wimbledon had assumed an international character and in 1905 May Sutton of the United States became the first champion from overseas when she won the Ladies' Singles. She repeated her success in 1907, the year when Norman Brookes of Australia became

An aerial view of the Worple Road Ground in 1921. The following year the All England Lawn Tennis Club moved to the present ground in Church Road.

The Centre Court at Worple Road in 1892.

the first Gentlemen's Singles champion from overseas. Since that year only two players from Great Britain, Arthur Gore and Fred Perry, have managed to win the event. Anthony Wilding of New Zealand became champion from 1910–1913 and as the war clouds gathered over Europe, Norman Brookes regained the title.

When Wimbledon resumed in 1919 a new generation of players sought honours. Suzanne Lenglen of France ended Britain's 35 years' dominance of the Ladies' Singles when she defeated the holder, Dorothea Lambert Chambers, in the Challenge Round. Norman Brookes returned to defend his crown but was no match for his fellow-countryman, Gerald Patterson. The next year heralded the arrival of Bill Tilden of the United States, reckoned by many as the greatest player in the history of the game.

A New Home

Prior to the First World War the facilities at Worple Road were expanded to meet the ever growing demand of the public and a move to larger premises was planned. This was not achieved until 1922 when the present ground in Church Road was opened by King George V. The foresight of building the present stadium, designed to hold 14,000 people, did more to popularise the game world wide than anything else that has happened to date.

The new ground, which many thought would turn out to be a "white elephant", was financed partly from the accumulated reserves of the Club and partly by the issue of Debentures. Misgivings about the future popularity of The Championships were soon dispelled and applications for tickets in the first year were such that they had to be issued by ballot – a system that has been adopted for every Championship since.

The move to Church Road coincided with a break in tradition, whereby the Challenge Round was abolished in favour of the holder playing through each round.

Wimbledon Thrives

Each year during the twenties, France produced at least one singles champion. Towards the end of Suzanne Lenglen's reign the famous 'Four Musketeers', Jean Borotra, Jacques Brugnon, Henri Cochet and Rene Lacoste, appeared on the scene and during the next ten years won six singles and five doubles titles between them. Britain's Kitty McKane (Godfree) won the Ladies' Singles in 1924 and 1926 and a year later Helen Wills of the United States started her conquest.

Wimbledon continued to thrive in the thirties. Bill Tilden returned at the age of 38 to gain his third crown and in 1931 Cilly Aussem registered Germany's first win in the Ladies' Singles. The following year over 200,000 spectators were present for the first time.

The years from 1934 to 1937 were a golden era for British tennis, when a total of 11 titles were captured, including three singles in succession by Fred Perry and two by Dorothy Round. During the same period Great Britain successfully defended the Davis Cup three times in Challenge Rounds staged on the Centre Court. The years just before the Second World War belonged to the United States. Donald Budge won all three events in 1937 and 1938, Helen Wills Moody captured the Ladies' Singles for the eighth time and Alice Marble brought a new dimension to ladies' tennis with her serve and volley game.

Wartime Wimbledon

During the Second World War the Club managed to remain open despite severe curtailment of staff. The premises were used for a variety of civil defence and military functions such as fire and ambulance services, Home Guard and a decontamination unit. Troops stationed within the vicinity were allowed to use the main concourse for drilling. Another familiar sight around the ground was a small farmyard consisting of pigs, hens, geese, rabbits, etc. In October 1940 a 'stick' of five 500lb bombs straddled the Club, the second of which struck the Centre Court roof and resulted in the loss of 1,200 seats.

Wimbledon at War. In 1940 a bomb struck the Centre Court and resulted in the loss of 1,200 seats.

With the war in Europe over, signs of normality began to return to Wimbledon during June and July, 1945, when a series of matches between Allied servicemen took place on the old No. 1 Court, which had escaped enemy action. During August the final stages of the United States European Championships were played and Charles Hare, an Englishman serving in the U.S. Army, became champion.

Play Resumed

Early in 1946 the decision was taken to resume The Championships that summer. The monumental task of organising the meeting in so short a time was entrusted to Lt. Col. Duncan Macaulay, the newly appointed Secretary. With unlimited enthusiasm he overcame a multitude of problems created by the rationing of almost every commodity, available only by licence, permit or coupon. Much of the war damage was cleared and repairs carried out in an attempt to get the ground back to normal – a situation not achieved until 1949 when building restrictions were eased.

The Post-War Period

The American dominance of Wimbledon, which began before the war, continued well into the fifties. Outstanding among an array of champions were Jack Kramer, Ted Schroeder, Tony Trabert, Louise Brough, Maureen Connolly and Althea Gibson, the first black winner.

From 1956 until the early seventies the Gentlemen's Singles was virtually the property of Australia and Lew Hoad, Neale Fraser, Rod Laver, Roy Emerson and John Newcombe became household names. The sequence of American wins in the Ladies' Singles was not broken until 1959, when graceful Maria Bueno of Brazil triumphed. In the next decade Margaret Smith became the first Australian to win the event, while Angela Mortimer and Ann Jones revived the British interest.

Open Tennis

The expansion of air travel in the fifties resulted in a great increase in the number of foreign players at Wimbledon and other tournaments throughout the world, but with this new era came an epidemic of what had become known as "shamateurism" – the receiving by amateur players of financial assistance in excess of amounts permitted by the International Tennis Federation – the authority in charge of the rules of lawn tennis and the governing body of the game world-wide.

The need for reform was evident. The initiative came from the Club, led by the then Chairman, Herman David, who in late 1959 put forward a proposal to The Lawn Tennis Association that The Championships be made open to all players. The following July the ITF rejected this move and several years followed in which argument persisted at all levels of the game. In 1964 the Club tried to persuade the LTA unilaterally to declare The Championships "open" but support was not forthcoming.

In August 1967 an invitation tournament for men (sponsored by the B.B.C. to mark the introduction of colour television) was held on the Centre Court, with eight players taking part – all professionals. Most of these players had won honours at Wimbledon in their amateur days but had forfeited the right to play there on turning professional. The segregation of the two categories was soon to come to an end.

In December that year the Annual Meeting of the LTA voted over-whelmingly to admit players of all categories to Wimbledon and other tournaments in Britain. Faced with a *fait accompli* the ITF yielded and allowed each nation to determine its own legislation regarding amateur and professional players. In 1968 Rod Laver and Billie Jean King became the first Wimbledon Open champions. The total prize money that year was £26,150.

The Boycott

1973 was a sad year for Wimbledon as 81 members of the Association of Tennis Professionals boycotted the meeting following the suspension earlier in the year of Nikki Pilic by the Yugoslavian Lawn Tennis Association. Despite the absence of so many top class players the attendance reached over 300,000. Jan Kodes of Czechoslovakia became champion in company with Billie Jean King of the United States, who won the Ladies' Singles for the sixth time.

Records Broken

In recent years long-standing records have been broken. In 1980 Bjorn Borg of Sweden became the first player to win the Gentlemen's Singles five times in succession since the 1880s. In 1985 Boris Becker became the youngest player, the first unseeded player, and the first German to win the Gentlemen's Singles. In 1987 Martina Navratilova of the United States became the first player to win the Ladies' Singles six times in succession and in 1990 attained the all-time record of nine victories in the event. Pete Sampras of the United States registered his seventh win in 2000.

Anniversary Celebrations

In 1977 The Championships celebrated their centenary. On the opening day forty-one out of fifty-two surviving singles champions paraded on the Centre Court and each received a silver commemorative medal from H.R.H. The Duke of Kent, the President of the Club, to mark the occasion. On the second Friday, The Championships were honoured by the presence of H.M. The Queen who presented the Ladies' Singles trophy to Virginia Wade on the Centre Court, together with a special trophy to mark Her Majesty's Silver Jubilee. As part of the celebrations The Wimbledon Lawn Tennis Museum and Kenneth Ritchie Wimbledon Library were opened.

The centenary of the Ladies' Singles Championship was celebrated in 1984. The highlight of The Championships was the parade on the Centre Court of 17 out of 20 surviving champions, who each received a unique piece of Waterford Crystal from H.R.H. The Duke of Kent.

The 100th Championships in 1986 were celebrated in a variety of ways, including a special Dinner Party for those who had made significant contributions to The Championships over the years, and the formation of the Last 8 Club. 1993 marked the 100th Ladies' Championships and the occasion was suitably commemorated.

The occasion of the Millennium was celebrated on the first Saturday when 64 Singles' Champions, Doubles Champions four or more times, and Singles Finalists at least twice, paraded on the Centre Court.

The Ever Changing Scene

Over the years the Club has constantly been aware of the need to provide facilities and ground improvements compatible with the pace and demand of modern day sport. Seldom has a year gone by without alteration to the ground or some organisational change taking place. In recent years the momentum has increased and major works programmes have provided improved facilities for the players, spectators, officials and media.

In 1979 the roof of the Centre Court was raised one metre to provide room for another 1,088 seats. The same year a new Debenture Holders' Lounge was constructed on the north side of the Centre Court. In 1980 the Members' Enclosure was made a permanent building. The following year the old No. 1 Court complex was rebuilt and enlargements to the North and South Stands increased the capacity of the court by 1,250.

Aorangi (Cloud in the sky) Park was brought into the perimeter of the Club's grounds in 1982 to give more room during The Championships.

A view of the All England Lawn Tennis Club, during The Championships of 1959

The East Side Building of the Centre Court was opened in 1985. In 1986 a new pavilion in Aorangi Park was built.

In 1991 the Centre Court North Building was extended northwards to provide greater accommodation for the Debenture Holders' Lounge, Museum offices, stores and Library and Club facilities. A mammoth operation in 1992 replaced the Centre Court roof by a new structure, supported by four pillars, instead of 26. 3,601 seats were given a perfect, instead of restricted, view.

Wimbledon into the 21st Century

Wimbledon is acknowledged to be the premier tennis tournament in the world and the priority of The All England Lawn Tennis Club, which hosts The Championships, is to maintain its leadership into the twenty first century. To that end a Long Term Plan was unveiled in 1993, which improved the quality of the event for spectators, players, officials and neighbours.

Stage one. The Plan was completed for the 1997 Championships and involved building in Aorangi Park the new No. 1 Court, a Broadcast Centre, two extra grass courts and a tunnel under the hill linking Church Road and Somerset Road.

Stage two. Involved the removal of the old No. 1 Court complex to make way for the new Millennium Building and the extension of the West Stand of the Centre Court with 728 extra seats.

Stage three. The opening of the new Museum Building, followed by the development of the new Centre Court East and North Buildings, increased the seating capacity to 15,000 and provided a retractable roof by the 2009 Championships. The modernisation of the Centre Court was complete. A new No. 2 Court, seating 4,000 people was opened in 2009 and in 2011 a new No. 3 Court, seating 2000 people, and new No. 4 Court were brought into operation and this saw the completion of the original Long Term Plan.

In the autumn of 2011 The Club announced a new Long Term Plan named Wimbledon 2020, which will redevelop areas of the ground which were not part of the original plan.

Milestones of Wimbledon

1868 Club founded as 'The All England Croquet Club" in Worple Road, Wimbledon.

1875 Lawn tennis first played at Club.

1877 Spencer Gore won the first Lawn Tennis Championships staged.

1884 Ladies' Singles and Gentlemen's Doubles events introduced into The Championships.

1887 Lottie Dod of Great Britain, aged 15, became the youngest winner of the Ladies' Singles.

1889 William Renshaw of Great Britain won the Gentlemen's Singles for the seventh time.

1902 Two matches were required to decide the Ladies' Singles challenge round.

1905 May Sutton of the United States became the first overseas singles champion.

1907 The Prince of Wales (later King George V) visited The Championships and accepted the first Presidency of the Club. Norman Brookes of Australia became the first overseas winner of the Gentlemen's Singles.

1909 New Club colours of dark green and purple introduced.

1913 Ladies' Doubles and Mixed Doubles events added to the programme.

1919 All five titles won by overseas players.

1920 Suzanne Lenglen of France became the first player to win three titles in a year.

1922 Club moved to present site in Church Road and opened by King George V. Challenge rounds abolished.

1924 Simple form of seeding introduced. A public ticket ballot was held for the first time.

1926 The Jubilee Championships. All surviving Singles and Gentlemen's Doubles champions attending received commemorative medals from King George V and Queen Mary on the Centre Court.

1927 First radio broadcast. Full seeding introduced. Billie Tapscott of South Africa became the first woman to play without wearing stockings.

1932 Over 200,000 spectators attended.

1937 Donald Budge of the United States became the first man to win three titles in one year. First television transmission.

1938 Helen Moody of the United States won the Ladies' Singles for the eighth time.

1947 Jack Kramer of the United States was the first singles champion to wear shorts. Junior singles events instituted for boys and girls.

1957 Queen Elizabeth attended the meeting. Althea Gibson of the United States became first black champion.

1962 Queen Elizabeth attended the meeting.

1964 Veterans' event started.

1967 Over 300,000 spectators attended the meeting. The first professional tournament (for eight players) staged a few weeks after The Championships to celebrate the introduction of B.B.C. colour television transmissions.

1968 The Championships made "open" to all players.

1971 Tie-break system of scoring introduced.

1973 Nearly 80 men members of the Association of Tennis Professionals boycotted the meeting following the suspension of Nikki Pilic by his Yugoslavian Lawn Tennis Association for failing to play in a Davis Cup match.

1977 The Centenary Championships. Queen Elizabeth attended the meeting. Past Singles champions presented with commemorative medals on the Centre Court by the Duke and Duchess of Kent. Wimbledon Lawn Tennis Museum and Kenneth Ritchie Wimbledon Library opened.

1979 The roof of the Centre Court was raised to provide extra seating. Billie Jean King of the United States won record 20th title at The Championships.

1980 Four new grass courts brought into commission. Bjorn Borg of Sweden won the Gentlemen's Singles for the fifth successive year.

1981 The old No. 1 Court South Stand was replaced by a new building.

1982 Sunday play scheduled. Development of Aorangi Park.

1983 Ladies' Singles draw increased to 128.

1984 The Centenary of the Ladies' Singles Championship.

1985 New Centre Court East Side Building. Boris Becker of West Germany, aged 17, became the youngest winner of the Gentlemen's Singles.

1986 The 100th Championships. Over 400,000 spectators attended the meeting. New Aorangi Park pavilion.

1990 A safety certificate from the local authority was necessary for the Centre and old No. 1 Court complex. Increased safety standards brought about many changes, including the Centre Court being an all-seater stadium. Martina Navratilova won the Ladies' Singles for a record ninth time.

1991 Centre Court North Building extended to accommodate new Debenture Holders' Lounge.

1992 New Centre Court roof supported by only four pillars.

1993 The 100th Ladies' Championships. Total refurbishment of the old No. 1 Court Competitors' Complex. The Club announced their Long Term Plan to enhance and protect The Championships pre-eminence into the next century. The Club purchased the freehold of the Wimbledon Park Golf Club.

1997 Opening of the new No. 1 Court, No. 18 and No. 19 Courts, Broadcast Centre and a tunnel linking Church Road with Somerset Road.

1999 Centre Court West Stand extension increased the seating capacity of the court by 728 to 13,813.

2000 Millennium Building, providing facilities for competitors, press, officials and Members, opened. Millennium Parade on Centre Court. Pete Sampras of United States won Gentlemen's Singles for seventh time.

2002 Complete refurbishment of Clubhouse.

2005 New Museum Building opened.

2007 Equal prize money for Ladies' and Gentlemen's events.

2008 New Centre Court East and North Building extensions opened. Fixed Roof in place. Court capacity raised to over 15,000 people.

2009 New No. 2 Court and Centre Court Retractable Roof fully operational. The modernisation of the Centre Court was complete. Over 500,000 spectators attended the meeting.

2010 John Isner (USA) and Nicolas Mahut (FRA) contested record match of 183 games, lasting 11 hours, 5 mins.

2011 New No. 3 Court, seating 2,000 people and new No. 4 Court opened.

Facilities available to Spectators

Banking

There is a sub-branch of HSBC at the north end of the Museum Building, at Gate 3, which transacts all usual banking business from the ground, opening until 8 p.m. on each day of The Championships.

Car Parking

There are seven official car parks situated adjacent to the Club. No. 3 is to the west, with an entrance in Somerset Road. No. 4 is to the north, with an entrance in Somerset Road. No. 5 (Wimbledon Club) and Nos. 6 and 8 (Wimbledon Park Golf Club) are to the east with entrances in Church Road also in Home Park for No. 6. No. 10 (Wimbledon Park operated by the London Borough of Merton) is to the north-east, with an entrance in Wimbledon Park Road.

Car Park Nos. 3, 5 and 8 may be reserved. Car Park No. 4 (coaches and motor cycles only), 6 and 10 are unreserved.

There is a Park and Ride service operating at Morden Park. Car parking is £15.00 per car, with no charge for the bus ride.

The AA office is situated in Car Park 4, off Somerset Road, inside Gate 20.

Catering

Wimbledon is the largest single annual sporting catering operation carried out in Europe. All the catering for The Championships is in the hands of Facilities Management Catering Limited.

Spectators are catered for from 10.30 a.m. every day on the Tea Lawn, east of Centre Court and in the No. 1 Court Stadium. Along one side of the Tea Lawn is 200 feet of counter space, where beer, soft drinks, tea, coffee and snacks are served. On the other side are strawberries and cream, Pimm's and champagne, pizzas, baguettes and Dutchees.

The Wingfield Restaurant is the only public, bookable restaurant and offers lunch and afternoon tea. Reservations for lunch can be made online at www.fmccatering.co.uk. The Courtside and Champions' Room located in Centre Court, are for the exclusive use of Centre Court Debenture Holders, and offer an à la carte menu and an all inclusive drinks package, respectively. Situated in No. 1 Court for use by Debenture Holders only are three restaurants: the Renshaw, which offers a drinks-inclusive luncheon and afternoon tea; The Veranda, an exciting concept of Alfresco modern dining offering a fixed-price Italian lunch menu, and the No. 1 Bar which is situated on the balcony of The Lounge (formerly the No. 1 Debenture Holders Restaurant) offering champagne, wine, draught and bottled beers, Pimm's, and coffee plus salads and a limited range of sandwiches.

Reservations, for The Renshaw only, can be made by emailing reservations. fmc@aeltc.com

There are two self-service restaurants, Café Pergola and the Conservatory Kitchen, offering a range of hot and cold meals and light refreshments. The Baseline Diner and Cafe also provide an informal setting, offering a selection of hot and cold meals. The Food Village provides a wide range of refreshments including oriental stir fry, fish and chips, burgers, pizzas, cookies, ice cream, beverages and the Village Bar. The Aorangi Food Court offering light refreshments including strawberries, and the Aorangi Café serving Southern-fried chicken and wine in addition to light refreshments and other beverages are adjacent to the Aorangi Terrace where Pimm's and ice cream are also available.

Members of the Club and Council Members of The Lawn Tennis Association together with their guests use the Members' Enclosure. Officials of the County Lawn Tennis Associations, Debenture Holders, umpires and stewards, the press, competitors, ball boys and girls and television broadcasters all have their own catering facilities.

About 1,800 FMC catering staff are required to operate these outlets and the quantity of food and drink served by them during the fortnight is enormous. Typical examples are: 12,000 kilos of poached and smoked salmon; 28,000 kilos of English strawberries; 32,000 portions of fish and chips; 6,000 stone-baked pizzas; 190,000 sandwiches; 135,000 ice creams; 300,000 cups of tea and coffee; 250,000 bottles of water; 30,000 litres of milk; 7,000 litres of dairy cream, a combined total of 150,000 Bath buns, scones, pastries and doughnuts; 200,000 glasses of Pimm's; 100,000 pints of draught beer and lager and 25,000 bottles of champagne. In addition, over 207,000 lunches are served, as well as 30,000 meals for FMC's own staff.

Chemist Shop

Lloyds Pharmacy provide a shop facility in the No. 1 Court Stadium.

Cushions

A souvenir cushion may be purchased daily at the grounds from 'Wimbledon Shop' outlets.

First Aid

For spectators the arrangements are in the hands of the St. John Ambulance Brigade. Four First Aid Posts are positioned in the grounds: an HQ Post at Gate 7, two in the Centre Court Building and one in the No. 1 Court Stadium. Doctors are in attendance every day in case of illness or injury.

Information Service

A wide variety of information is available from Information Desks situated around the grounds.

Left Luggage and Lost Property

All Left Luggage facilities are outside the grounds, in Wimbledon Park, on the Wimbledon Park Golf Course and in Car Park 1. Items may be left at these facilities for £1.00 per item (with a charge of £5.00 for camping equipment)

A Lost Property Office is situated underneath the West Stand of No. 3 Court.

Telephone enquiries about items left in the grounds should be made to 020 8971 2251. All items must be claimed by 30th September of the relevant Championships year.

Live@Wimbledon

A radio and online television channel, based in the Broadcast Centre, designed for internet distribution on www.wimbledon.com and offering live coverage of play, match reports, behind-the-scenes interviews and features, details on the facilities in the Grounds, traffic conditions and weather reports.

The online television channel, launched in 2012 is available for audiences in the UK and the USA. The radio service, which first went on air in 1992, is available worldwide on the internet and for the local community within a radius of four miles of the Club, on three FM services. The main service is on 87.7FM while full commentary of the matches on Centre and No. 1 Courts is available on 96.3FM and 97.8FM respectively, to enable spectators with a visual or hearing disability to follow play more easily.

Lost Persons

Any spectator who may have lost contact with a relation or friend should make enquiries at the Information Kiosk at the South West corner of the Centre Court in St. Mary's Walk, up to 7 p.m. and thereafter at the Church Road Entrance at Gate 5.

Official Programme

Programmes of The Championships are sold inside and outside the grounds during the meeting. They are the only official programmes and can be obtained from the stands of Programme Publications Ltd., and their sellers.

Programmes can be sent by post on application to the Club at the current price, plus postage, both just before and during the Meeting.

Applications for the purchase of completed programmes, giving the results of all matches including the finals, may be made during the Fortnight at the office of Programme Publications Ltd., situated underneath the No. 3 Court, or to the Club at the conclusion of The Championships.

Picnics

The Aorangi Terrace is provided with tables and chairs, where picnics may be taken.

Police

A Metropolitan Police office is located in the North Hall of the Centre Court.

Post Office Facilities

Main Post Office services are not provided within the grounds, but postage stamps etc, are obtainable from the Newsagents situated east of No.1 Court. A post box is also available outside the Newsagents.

Retail and Information Kiosks

A number of kiosks, situated east of the No. 1 Court Stadium, include the following services: Banking services, Match Statistics, Wimbledon Shop, Newsagents and Pharmacy.

Scoreboards

Electronic repeater scoreboards for spectators to follow the progress of matches on Centre and No. 1 Courts are positioned on either side of the clock above the Main Entrance to the Clubhouse, on the west wall of the Centre Court and at the entrance to the South-West Hall of the No. 1 Court. All show the score point by point.

There are electronic scoreboards overlooking the south concourse, opposite the Café Pergola and on the north wall of the Press Centre which display current scores of matches on court. The main scoreboards for spectators to follow the progress of matches, are located on the Debenture Holders' Lounge wall facing Nos. 14, 15 and 16 Courts and inside the Championships Entrance at Gate 3. These show the full draw of each of the five Championship events, which are updated as soon as the matches are completed. The order of play is also shown. Electronic Match Information Displays, positioned on the south-west wall of the Centre Court, another facing out from No. 1 Court towards Aorangi Pavilion and a third on the Tea Lawn, show the latest point by point score for every match on all 19 courts in use.

Telephones

Public telephones are located inside the grounds at the Lost Property Office (near Gate 13), in the Centre Court (North-East), in the No. 1 Court Stadium (South-East) and outside the grounds near Gate 9 and in Marryat Road.

Television Screen

Because spectators with ground-only tickets are unable to follow matches on the Centre Court and other show courts, a 142 sq feet television screen, may be

Aorangi Terrace packed with spectators watching the action on the giant television screen, adjacent to No. 1 Court.

17

On the Riviera: The Museum's special exhibition follows racket-laden tourists to the sundrenched South of France.

viewed from the Aorangi Terrace. Approximately 3,000 people at a time are able to watch the action. Seats are provided for 214 people.

Tennis Promotions

'Play Tennis' organised by the LTA, is operating daily, adjacent to No. 12 Court, and features themed interactive tennis areas to introduce youngsters to tennis in a fun way that inspires and motivates them to play. There is also a small refreshment facility and the 'Speed of Serve'.

On the first Saturday in Wimbledon Park, the Lawn Tennis Association, the London Borough of Merton and the All England Lawn Tennis Club are arranging a fun weekend of tennis for aspiring young tennis players.

A player Autograph and Interview Island is available adjacent to the Aorangi Pavillion.

Toilets

Public toilets are situated in the grounds, in the Centre Court building, the No. 1 Court Stadium, inside Gate 12, east and south of the No. 2 Court Stadium, south of the new No. 3 Court Stadium and at the south end of the grounds. There are also public toilets in Car Parks Nos. 4 (near Gate 20) and 10, the bus terminus and the golf course off Wimbledon Park Road.

Travel Information

The nearest stations to the ground are Southfields (Underground – District Line) and Wimbledon (British Rail and Underground – District Line). Special bus services and taxis run between these stations and the ground. Spectators leaving the ground requiring a bus or taxi should queue in Church Road for Southfields and in Somerset Road for Wimbledon.

Wimbledon on the Web

Since 1995, information about the Club and The Championships has been available to users on the Internet originally at www.wimbledon.org.

The Internet site contains information about the Club and the history of Wimbledon. During The Championships it contains a wealth of information including current point-by-point scores, statistics, news, photos and videos. The site also carried live Radio Wimbledon giving computer users around the world the opportunity to listen to live commentary on matches and to receive the latest news. Also included is the Wimbledon shop where visitors are able to make an electronic purchase from the limited range of Championships merchandise.

In 2000 mobile phone users from around the world were able to register with the website, allowing them to receive match results for their favourite players and news during The Championships.

An added service in 2000 and extended for 2001 was the WAP service. This allowed users to browse key pages of the website from their mobile phones, including the order of play and point by point scores.

In 2006, mobile phone users were able to receive updates via their service providers. In some cases this included live video of matches.

New in 2006 was the ability to watch live match play on www. wimbledon.org. Prior to 2006 users had been able to watch archive material and match highlights. In 2006 via a subscription service in most parts of the world, users could access multiple live matches on up to nine show courts. This service was repeated in 2007 and 2008. From 2009, a new m. wimbledon.org site provided an optimised experience for fans looking at the world wide web from their mobile phone. IBM also developed the first Grand Slam iPhone 'app' including point-by-point scores, video, news, schedules and results. There were over 890,000 iphone downloads and 640,000 Android downloads during The Championships 2012, bringing the Wimbledon experience to new global audience. Social networking sites such as Facebook and Twitter also grew in popularity, bringing users an alternative view of The Championships.

From 2009, the Club worked with our broadcast partners around the world to provide access to live play as well as highlights and archive material on our website. In 2011, coinciding with the 125th Anniversary of The Championships the website launched as www.wimbledon.com. In 2012 the website relaunched with a completely new design; in addition to scores, schedules and player data, the site makes use of some iconic photography about the grounds and The Championships. From 2012 the year-round and Championships websites were combined into a single site, hosted in the IBM Cloud. The website also hosted the live@Wimbledon service, including analysis and interviews, plus a limited view of some live tennis action, as well as the radio commentaries previously distributed as Radio Wimbledon.

Wimbledon Shops

Wimbledon merchandise is sold in three main shops in the grounds, on the south east corner of Centre Court, on the ground floor of the No. 1

Court Complex and in the Museum Building by Gate 3. In addition, there is a series of kiosks situated around the grounds for spectators to purchase souvenir items. Kiosks are to be found by the giant television screen on the Aorangi Terrace, by St Mary's Walk, by Gate 1, behind Court 15, in front of the Aorangi Pavilion, Gate 13 opposite No. 4 Court and on the corner of No. 2 Court by Gate 7. There are also two kiosks, one selling tennis books and postcards and other souvenir items by Gate 3. The shops are open daily during The Championships from ground opening to close of play, except on the final Sunday, when Sunday trading hours apply.

Wimbledon Lawn Tennis Museum

The original Wimbledon Lawn Tennis Museum was opened by H.R.H. The Duke of Kent in 1977 as part of the Centenary celebrations. The construction of the Centre Court East Side Building in 1984/5 led to the design of a completely new Museum, in which more of the expanding collection could be seen.

In 1993 H.R.H. The Duke of Kent consented to become Patron and during 1994 visited the Museum.

The announcement in 2002 of the Club's plans for a roof on Centre Court and the redevelopment of the East Side necessitated the removal of the Museum and all its associated activities. A new Museum, designed by Mather & Company and housed in the Museum Building, was opened on 12th April 2006 by H.R.H. The Duke of Kent.

The Museum contains historic galleries, themed galleries devoted to tennis equipment and tennis fashions, and zones focussing on tennis today and life on the circuit. The Museum employs new technology with a variety of interactives, easy-to-use touchscreens, and audioguides in ten languages. Highlights include the 'ghost' of John McEnroe who appears in the Gentlemen's Dressing Room, and a newly-installed 3D cinema featuring the film *Viewpoint*.

In September 2009, CentreCourt360, a glass viewing platform together with interactive displays, was installed for the first time. Open to all Museum visitors, out of Championships, it is accessed through the Wingfield Cafe. In autumn 2010, tactile drawings with Braille, highlighting aspects of Centre Court, were introduced for partially-sighted as well as sighted visitors.

Early in 2011, a new interactive was developed giving visitors the opportunity to engage with objects in the Museum's store, and a display highlighting the Longest Match between John Isner and Nicolas Mahut was installed.

During 2012, a special exhibition devoted to tennis and the Olympic Games ran throughout the year, and was updated after the 2012 Olympic and Paralympic tennis events were held.

In April 2013, a new exhibitoin On the *Riviera: Tennis in the South of France 1874–1939* was installed in the Museum Gallery.

Following The Championships 2005, the Museum Education Department moved to No.1 Court. Over the past year, more than 7,500 students have attended activities run by Museum Education. The programme caters for stu-

The Lawn Tennis Museum Library - open to the public for 50 weeks of the year.

dents from five years of age to post-graduate level and consists of workshops, lectures and themed tours of the grounds.

Demand for behind-the-scenes tours of The All England Lawn Tennis Club has again been unprecedented. Tours can be organised for pre-booked groups in 14 languages. Public tours led by Blue Badge guides for individual visitors are also available and there is an online booking service.

The Wimbledon Shop at the Museum sells a wide range of Wimbledon leisurewear, gifts and DVDs. Museum publications, highlighting the history of Wimbledon and aspects of the collections, are available from the Shop.

The Museum is open during The Championships from 9.30a.m.–8.00p.m. (or close of play if earlier). Throughout the year, the Museum is open daily from 10.00a.m. to 5.30p.m. (beginning April to end September), and 10.00a.m. to 5.00p.m. (beginning October to end March) with the exception of the following days:

- Closed the Sunday immediately prior to The Championships, the middle Sunday of The Championships, the Monday immediately after The Championships (unless there is play) and the Tuesday after the Championships
- Christmas Eve, Christmas Day, Boxing Day and New Year's Day.

Further details of opening times and tour bookings are obtainable on 020 8946 6131 or museum@aeltc.com or from the website www.wimbledon.com/museum.

The Wingfield Café is available to visitors for refreshments throughout the year, excluding The Championships.

The Kenneth Ritchie Wimbledon Library, which is part of the Wimbledon Lawn Tennis Museum, contains an outstanding collection of British and foreign lawn tennis books, annuals, programmes, and other ephemera which is available to the public for study and research. Admission is by appointment. Normally the Library is open Monday to Friday but is closed to the public during The Championships.

Interesting facts and figures

Advertising

The Championships are advertised in the national press, lawn tennis publications and via posters at certain underground and railway stations, at intervals from October onwards.

The Order of Play is published each day in national newspapers and on line, as well as in the Wimbledon Programme.

Attendance

Attendance figures from the early days at Church Road are not known but in 1932 over 200,000 spectators were present for the first time. This number gradually increased to over 250,000 in 1956 and to over 300,000 in 1967 and the 400,000 barrier was broken for the first time in 1986. The record attendance for the meeting is 511,043 in 2009. The record attendance for one day stands at 46,826 on the first Wednesday of 2009.

Broadcast Centre

This is the thirteenth year for the worlds leading broadcasters to use the purpose-built, 5,000 sq.metre, Broadcast Centre which was opened for the 1997 Championships. It continues to provide a range of facilities unmatched by any other sporting organisation, and the days of working from what used to be called a shanty town are now a distant, but fond memory.

Coin Tossing Ceremony

In 2000 an innovation was introduced whereby two youngsters performed a coin tossing ceremony prior to the Gentlemen's and Ladies' Singles Finals. They are nominated on behalf of charities.

Competitors' Amenities

There are separate blocks of seats on the Centre Court and No. 1 Court provided for competitors and each is allowed to have a limited number of guest passes. Competitors are transported in chauffeur-driven cars to and from the ground each day. A restaurant is provided for competitors where they can obtain lunch and tea and where they can take their guests for tea. A room is provided for rest and relaxation between matches and where players can meet their agents, etc.

In each dressing room physiotherapy is available. There are 14 official physiotherapists in attendance during The Championships. A gymnasium is also available for competitors.

Curtailment of Play

The Centre Court retractable roof was operational for the first time at the 2009 Championships and is used within a set of guidelines laid down to meet the different weather conditions. The Wimbledon Programme contains details of these guidelines.

In the event of rain all other courts are covered. Play is resumed as soon as possible but often the start is delayed owing to damp caused by condensation under the covers.

A view overlooking No. 10 and No. 11 Courts with No. 2 Court in the background. The spire of St Mary's Church can be seen in the distance.

Gardens

Each year the gardeners strive to bring the landscapes of the AELTC to ever higher standards. With the traditions brought to the Club by Natural Green since the early 1950's, Natural Green seek out ever more imaginative ways to complement the tennis site with landscaping, flowers, and thoughtful planting schemes. Natural Green will be selecting and planting a wide variety of themed flowers, hanging baskets and individually planted displays throughout the site. Traditional colour schemes cascade from window boxes, topiary plants are clipped, and a sea of blues, white, purples and greens will be there to welcome each visitor. Natural Green source where ever possible from local growers and British suppliers to create the Wimbledon look.

Hospitality Facilities

Hospitality facilities are provided on the Club's hard courts and in Suites in the Centre and No. 1 Court Stadiums.

International Box

The International Box, situated in the North Open Stand of the Centre Court, has some 86 seats reserved for representatives of international tennis associations. There are also 20 seats reserved in No. 1 Court.

The International Tennis Federation

During The Championships the administration office of the International Tennis Federation is situated in the North Hall of the Centre Court.

Last 8 Club

The Last 8 Club, inaugurated in 1986 as part of the 100th Championship celebrations, recognises the contribution made to lawn tennis by players who have reached the quarter-finals of the singles, the semi-finals of the Gentleman's and Ladies' Doubles or the final of the Mixed Doubles at The Championships. Each year the Chairman of the Club invites special guests from the membership of the Last 8 Club. The guests in 2013 are Jan Kodes, Victor Seixas, Margaret Court and Billie Jean King. A hospitality facility for the use of the Last 8 Club members is situated in a private suite adjacent to Gate 5.

The Lawn Tennis Association

During The Championships the administration offices of The Lawn Tennis Association are situated in the No. 1 Court Stadium, where there are also the British Tennis Membership and Sponsors' Suites.

Long Term Plan

In March 1993 the Committee of Management of The Championships unveiled its very ambitious Long Term Plan to take Wimbledon into the 21st Century. The plan was designed to protect the long term future of The Championships by improving the quality of the event for all involved – players, spectators, media, officials, members and neighbours and maintain the position as the world's premier tennis tournament.

Work commenced on 25th July 1994 and by the 2000 Championships, Stages 1 and 2 were completed, with the opening of the new No.1 Court Stadium, Broadcast Centre, No.18 and No.19 Courts, Centre Court West Building and Stand extension, tunnel connecting Church Road with Somerset Road, and the Millennium Building (on the site of the old No.1 Court), providing outstanding facilities for the players, media, officials and members.

The plan continued with the construction of a new building, housing office accommodation for Club Staff, the Wimbledon Lawn Tennis Museum and Library, Bank, Ticket Office and incorporating the Turnstile Entrance to the ground at Gate 3 commenced immediately after the 2003 Championships.

The No. 3 Court accomodates 1980 spectators of which 1494 are reserved seats.

View across No. 18 Court, with the Centre Court and Broadcast Centre in the background. The No. 1 Court can be seen to the left.

This was occupied by the end of 2005, and the new Museum opened in April 2006. This allowed the development of the Centre Court, including raising the capacity to 15,000, better facilities and a retractable roof. In addition new Nos. 2 to 4 Courts have been provided at the southern end of the grounds.

In the autumn of 2011 The Club announced a new Long Term Plan named 'Wimbledon 2020', which will redevelop areas of the ground which were not part of the original plan. Also, operational considerations may lead to the redevelopment of existing buildings to provide different facilities.

Players' Waiting Rooms

An official is responsible for ensuring that players are ready and waiting to go on the Centre and No. 1 Courts at the appropriate time. He also ensures that they are wearing the correct clothing as stated in the rules, both with regard to colour and advertising. The players are assembled in the Players' Waiting Room, which is underneath the Royal Box, until they are called.

Over the entrance to the Centre Court, through which the players pass, is the following inscription from Rudyard Kipling's poem 'If':
> "If you can meet with triumph and disaster
> And treat those two impostors just the same."

There are also Players' Waiting Rooms, situated in the No. 1 and No. 2 Courts.

Press, Radio and Photographers

In the past 10 years the average number of writers and international radio reporters attending The Championships has been around 725, drawn from 45 countries. Of these, almost 168 have full access to the Press Box and a further 220 or so have limited access. The remainder have full or day Rover passes which allow them to use the reserved press accommodation on the Show Courts and a variety of facilities, including a restaurant in the press area. On any given day the average number of press attending is 450–500.

The British press corps totals between 330–375, the figure often dependent on other major sporting events taking place at the same time as The Championships.

For example, in the year 2010, when the football World Cup coincided with The Championships, 333 British journalists were accredited: in 2008 when the football European Cup was being staged at the same time as Wimbledon, 317 British press were accredited. Most National newspapers and press agencies have up to 14 journalists attending – sport, features and news – and many journalists from provincial publications attend, particularly if a British player is local to them. The next country with the largest representation is the United States which averages 35–45 correspondents every year, followed by France, Italy, Japan, Germany and Switzerland who all have between 20–39 representatives amongst the press. Countries who have between 10–19 press include Australia, India, Russia Fed, The Netherlands, Poland, Spain and Belgium.

The number of press attending The Championships from a foreign country is usually reflected by the number of players from that particular country competing. In the year 2012, 600 journalists were accredited from 42 countries while 200 photographers' passes were issued from 108 International publications or agencies.

The International written press, radio reporters and photographers are housed on three floors in the Millennium Building, opened in 2000.

The Committee of Management maintains a close link with the press throughout the year and members of the Media Sub-Committee accompany players for the post match interviews – one of the traditions which makes Wimbledon unique among the Grand Slam events.

Prize Money

Prize money was first given when The Championships were made open to all categories of players in 1968. Over the years it has increased approximately 850 fold from the total of £26,150 in that year, when the Gentlemen's Singles Champion received £2,000 and the Ladies' Singles Champion £750. In 2007 equal prize money was given for the first time to the Gentlemen's and Ladies' events. The total prize money for 2013 is £22,560,000, with £1,600,000 going to each singles champion.

Radio and Television

Radio commentaries were first broadcast in 1927. Matches were first televised by the BBC in 1937 but it was not until after the Second World War that they were televised each day.

Situated along the top of the Centre Court are commentary boxes for almost 40 of the world's television networks, with several more positions for radio commentary boxes along the east side. Overlooking the No. 1 Court from the north end are 16 television and radio commentary boxes, while at ground level in the north-west corner are two BBC radio and television commentary boxes.

During The Championships in 2012 BBC TV Sports coverage of matches was the basis for televised programmes seen in 200 different territories.

Cameras covered play on nine courts, including Centre Court and No.1 Court. As host broadcaster, the BBC made a total of more than 1,000 hours of coverage available to international networks. Live play was also available via the Club Website.

Because of the growing overlap of terrestrial, cable and satellite broadcasters' transmissions footprints, it is impossible to calculate exact figures of the number of people who follow Wimbledon each year; but it is safe to say that it is seen by more people throughout the world than any other tennis tournament. This audience continues to grow as a result of the Club's agreements with a wide range of television stations.

In the United Kingdom the BBC transmitted over 250 hours of coverage on BBC1, BBC2 and the HD channel, including a daily highlights programme in the evening and many more hours on their digital interactive service and on-line.

In 2012, approximately 2,300 accreditations were processed for television and radio personnel covering The Championships.

Royal Box

The Royal Box, which seats 75 people, is used for the entertainment of guests from the Royal Family, the tennis world, including supporters of British tennis and other walks of life. Invitations come from the Chairman of the Club and the Committee of Management, taking into account suggestions from the committee members of the club, The Lawn Tennis Association and other sources. Guests are invited to lunch, tea and drinks at the end of the day, which take place within the clubhouse. Dress is smart, lounge suits/jacket and tie etc. Ladies are asked not to wear hats as they tend to obscure the vision of those seated behind them.

The Queen honoured the club with her presence in 1957, 1962, 1977 and 2010 and other members of the Royal Family are regular attendees.

Tennis Balls

About 54,250 balls are used on average during The Championships. New balls are supplied after seven games (to allow for the preliminary warm-up) and then after every nine games. Yellow balls were used for the first time in 1986. After use some balls are sold to clubs affiliated to The Lawn Tennis Association. Subject to availability, other balls are sold daily, from a kiosk positioned near No. 14 Court. The proceeds are donated to a Schools' tennis programme delivered by the Tennis Foundation.

Trophies

The winner of the Gentlemen's Singles Championship becomes the holder, for the year only of the "Challenge Cup", presented by The All England Lawn Tennis Club in 1887. The winner of the Ladies' Singles Championship becomes the holder, for the year only, of the "Challenge Trophy", a silver gilt salver, presented by The All England Lawn Tennis Club in 1886. The winners of the three doubles events become the holders, for the year only, of the cups. A silver salver is presented to the runners-up of all five events and a bronze medal to each semi-finalist. All trophies are kept permanently at the Club but winners receive three-quarter size trophies. Immediately the winners of the events are known the replicas are engraved, so enabling the players to leave The Championships with them in their possession.

Wimbledon Compendium, 2013

Further facts and figures regarding The Championships and The All England Lawn Tennis Club may be found in great depth in the above publication (572 pages), obtainable from the Wimbledon shops, price £16.00.

The All England Lawn Tennis and Croquet Club

Membership of the Club

Membership of the Club consists of five categories: (a) Full Members, (b) Life Members, (c) Honorary Members, (d) Temporary Members, (e) Junior Temporary Members. Members under headings (a), (b) and (c) are limited to 500 in number. Honorary Members include past singles champions, other eminent Lawn Tennis players, benefactors of the Club or The Championships, and other persons who have rendered special service to Lawn Tennis. Temporary Members are elected from year to year and generally are active players who make regular use of the Club and play in Club matches during their period of membership.

Club Grounds

The Club grounds consist of 19 grass courts (including the Centre Court and No. 1 Court), 8 American Clay courts and five indoor courts, two Greenset Velvelux and three Greenset Trophy. In Aorangi Park, there are 22 grass courts for practice before and during The Championships, and two green acrylic courts. The total area, including the Club's car parks, covers over 42 acres.

Club and Museum Staff

The permanent members of the Club office staff consist of Chief Executive, Championships Director, Finance Director, Marketing Director, Commercial Director, Information Technology Director, Club Secretary, Championships Director Designate and 57 other administrative staff.

There are 16 permanent members of the ground staff and a team of 35 buildings and services staff. The Dressing Rooms have a staff of six. Four members of the staff are engaged in the Wimbledon 2020 master plan.

The Museum has 10 permanent staff positions and six long term contract staff.

Use of Courts

Apart from the grass courts, the courts are used all year round by the Club members and LTA sponsored players. The grass courts are in play from May to September (except the Centre Court and other show courts which are used only for The Championships). The courts are lent to a number of clubs and organisations, mainly of a national character, for the staging of various events.

Due to changes in the world tennis calendar the Wightman Cup is no longer played – the last time the event was held at the Club was in 1972. Davis Cup ties take place at the Club occasionally. The last tie was against Austria on No. 1 Court in September, 2008.

Maintenance of Courts

The Centre Court and No. 1 Court are re-sown each year, where necessary, as soon as possible after The Championships. Contrary to popular belief, they are not re-turfed. The outside courts, although used considerably more throughout the year, are also oversown.

Court Capacity

The seating capacity of each court is as follows:-

Centre - 14,979	No. 7 - 120	No. 16 - 312
No. 1 - 11,393	No. 8 - 170	No. 17 - 309
No. 2 - 4,063	No. 12 - 1089	No. 18 - 782
No. 3 - 1982	No. 14 - 312	No. 19 - 302
No. 5 - 120	No. 15 - 318	

In addition, there are some 200 benches positioned around the outside courts providing seating for about 1,000. The capacity of the grounds is 38,500.

Consultants

The Club engages the International Management Group, who assist with a number of on-site agreements. They are responsible for television rights, the official film of The Championships and matters relating to merchandising.

A public relations consultancy "Johnny Perkins Associates Ltd" is retained to advise on and assist with all matters relating to communications with the press and public.

Landmarks

From 1931 until early in 2006 the wrought-iron Doherty Memorial Gates were situated at the main Church Road entrance to the ground. These were presented by the Rev. William Doherty in memory of his two younger brothers Laurie and Reggie, who dominated the game at the turn of the 20th century. The gates were moved to the southern end of the ground to allow new wider gates to be erected at the main entrance.

The pony roller was presented to the Club in 1872 by the then Secretary, John Walsh, on condition that his daughter was made a life member. In 1922 the roller was moved from Worple Road to the present ground and initially placed on the Centre Court. The roller was moved in 1924 to the newly opened old No. 1 Court, where it resided until late 1986. It is now located adjacent to the Broadcast Centre.

In 2007, the Water Tower, which had stood since 1922 was demolished as part of the Long Term Plan, south of the Centre Court. Originally the Tower was connected by pipeline to the Wimbledon Park Lake, east of the ground, but was seldom used due to technical difficulties. The ground floor was used as an incinerator. Initial designs of the Tower to incorporate a clock on each face were abandoned.

The Fred Perry statue was unveiled in 1984 to commemorate the 50th Anniversary of the first of his three victories in the Gentlemen's Singles Championship. The sculptor was David Wynne. Until March 2005 the statue was situated at the south concourse entrance to the Tea Lawn, when it was relocated to a site near the entrance to Café Pergola to allow future work to be carried out in connection with the modernization of the east side of the Centre Court. With the building works completed in March, 2010 the statue was relocated to the north-east corner of Centre Court, opposite the Museum entrance to the ground. The gates at the Somerset Road entrance to the ground were dedicated to Fred Perry, in 1984.

The weather-vane, situated on the roof of the Café Pergola, formerly the Members Enclosure, was presented to the Club in 1984 by Sir Brian Burnett, to mark his retirement as Chairman, 1974–1983.

Five head and shoulder sculptures of the British Ladies' Singles Champions who won their titles at Church Road, Kathleen McKane/Godfree, Dorothy Round,

The Centre Court accomodates 14,979 spectators.

Angela Mortimer, Ann Jones and Virginia Wade, are positioned at the entrance to the Clubhouse. They were unveiled by the players/relatives in April 2004. The sculptor was Ian Rank-Broadley.

The two cottages, No. 133 and No. 135 Somerset Road, located at the southern end of the grounds next to the west boundary wall, were the only existing structures from when the Club purchased the land for the present ground in 1921 and, consequently, were the oldest landmarks. Built before the First World War as farm cottages, the buildings were used by the Club over the years to accommodate various staff but were demolished in 2009.

'The All England Club's Junior Initiatives

In May 2001, the Club launched a series of junior initiatives, using the draw of the Wimbledon name to inspire children to play tennis.

There are three tenets to this scheme. The first is the Wimbledon Junior Tennis Initiative. WJTI, as it has become known as over the years, the Club's community tennis programme. It is run by Dan Bloxham, the AELTC Head Coach and his team of 15 coaches. At Easter 2013 Dan and his team had made 630 visits to state schools in Merton and Wandsworth. These visits have offered over 140,000 children a lively and constructive experience of tennis WJTI style!

Up to four children from each school visit can be selected to join the WJTI and attend the weekend coaching sessions which are held at the Club for 45 weeks a year. Around 4000 children have joined the WJTI and receive free coaching throughout their junior tennis career. During the course of a weekend up to 300 children will play tennis with Dan and the team. As the Initiative has developed the children who first started playing tennis with the WJTI have offered their help with the younger players and the eldest are now taking coaching exams and forming a significant part of the coaching team.

The WJTI Squad continues to offer the players with the greatest potential the opportunity to fully develop their game. The Squad trains for 49 weeks a year and compete with success at all levels and age groups from eight and under to 18 and under. In 2013 the WJTI has five teams in

The No.1 Court accommodates 11,393 spectators.

the AEGON Team Tennis competition, three of which are in the Premier Division for the first time. Strength and conditioning sessions are offered to the stronger Squad players with four players receiving individualised programmes. Eight WJTI players are currently receiving individual tennis lessons at a performance level, two of whom are national standard, six are regional and two are county standard.

One former Squad member is now at the University of SE Missouri on a full tennis scholarship and another is a member of the International Lawn Tennis Club of Great Britain.

The WJTI Squad "perform" on No. 14 Court on the middle Saturday and Final Sunday of The Championships where Dan shows how to grow a player with WJTI players from four years and upwards.

The second segment of the tennis initiative is the All England Club support and origination of the HSBC Road to Wimbledon National 14 & under Challenge which began in 2002 and is now since 2008 supported by the Championships Official banking partner HSBC.

Some 800 clubs and schools run their own Road to Wimbledon event each spring followed by 44 County Finals for those boys and girls who qualify and then 128 players qualify via the County Finals to the National Finals played at Wimbledon on grass annually each August.

Some juniors have rarely played on grass and many not been to Wimbledon so to qualify and play at the National Finals is a rare experience.

During the week the players, parents and coaches are taken around the historical grounds as well as visits to the museum and great experience playing on the Wimbledon lawns.

All the players have a minimum of five matches on the grass and the trophies and coaching grants as prizes are a good incentive for the best juniors who get to the finals.

The HSBC Road to Wimbledon is fully supported by the LTA whose county offices all over the country are involved in administering the county finals and encouraging clubs and schools to give their younger players an opportunity to compete in the event and who knows maybe qualify to play at Wimbledon.

The winners are then invited to the following year's Championships to attend the middle Saturday to a Tim Henman and Dan Bloxham tennis clinic before play starts alongside members of the Wimbledon WJTI.

The third element is the Wimbledon Lawn Tennis Museum's Education programme. Since starting in 2001, the Wimbledon Education department has seen over 39,000 students pass through its doors. In the past year over 7,500 students have participated in the Education Programme which provides curriculum based workshops and tours for 5 to 18 year olds, as well as lectures and tours for under- and postgraduate students. The Primary School Programme supports the National Curriculum subject areas of History, Art and Design, and Literacy. The Secondary School Programme has been developed to meet the needs of students studying for GCSE, BTEC and A-Level courses in Business Studies, Leisure and Tourism, and Physical Education. Bespoke packages have been designed for universities - both national and international – on the themes of marketing and sports management. All the tours and workshops ensure a unique and engaging learning experience for every student.

Finance

In 1920 The All England Lawn Tennis Ground Ltd. was formed (in 1996 the company became a plc) with the object of the Club purchasing and equipping a new ground at Wimbledon (present site) and with a view to raising capital by the issue of debentures and entering into a formal Agreement which would lock together the interests of the Club and The Lawn Tennis Association. The interlocking of the finances of The Championships between the Club, The Lawn Tennis Association and the Ground Company stems from an Agreement made in 1922, whereby the surplus from The Championships was shared between the Club and the LTA after paying the running expenses of the Club and deducting a preferential sum towards the redemption of debentures.

A revised Agreement made in 1934 provided, inter alia, for joint arrangements for managing The Championships instituted by the Club, mutual obligations in the event of a Championships financial deficiency and/or insufficiency, the transfer by the Club to the LTA of one half of its share holding in the Ground Company and the payment to the LTA of all the surplus arising from The Championships after meeting expenses incurred in running and administering the Club and the expenses of running The Championships (other than capital expenditure).

The 1934 Agreement was varied by a Deed of Variation in 1993 to give effect to changes appropriate to the circumstances in the 1990s and beyond: it will come to an end on 31st July, 2013. The Deed of Variation perpetuates the financial principles set out in the earlier Agreement, recognises the part played by the Club in staging The Championships and incorporates The All England Lawn Tennis Club (Wimbledon) Ltd. as the fourth party to the Agreement - a company formed for the purpose of exploiting commercially any trade marks, trade names etc. for the financial benefit of The Championships.

On 14th May 2009, the Club, the LTA and the Ground Company agreed arrangements for the continuation of their relationship in respect of The Championships for at least a further 40 years from 1st August 2013. Under a revised long term agreement, effective from that date, the Club will receive a 10% share of the surplus generated by The Championships. In addition, subject to certain conditions being satisfied, the Club will acquire the LTA's shares in the

Ground Company on 1st August 2013. The Championships will continue to be organised by the Committee of Management.

Every five years Centre Court debentures are sold to the public to raise additional funds for essential building work and major facility improvements at Wimbledon, including the current Long Term Plan. Such capital expenditure does not reduce the annual sum passed over to the LTA from each Championships. In return for their investment and support, debenture holders receive an entitlement to one Centre Court ticket per debenture (currently there are 2,500 debentures) for the five year period and the use of the debentures holders' restaurant, bars and other facilities. In recent years further funding has been provided by the issue of debentures for the new No. 1 Court. These debentures entitle the holder to a reserved seat for the first ten days of The Championship for each of the relevant years.

Croquet

Croquet was not provided for when the Club moved to the present Church Road ground and was first played in 1953. From 1st June, 1957 to 2nd September, 2007, a croquet lawn was situated at the southern end of the grounds alongside the Church Road boundary fence. The Club's Long Term Plan required other use for the lawn and a new lawn was created in the Southlands College ground, and was opened on 19th April, 2008. The Club Croquet Championships was re-introduced together with a Handicap singles event in 1960 and in recent years a golf croquet event was started.

Presidents of the Club

1907–1910	H.R.H. The Prince of Wales KG KT KP GCSI GCMG GCIE GCVO ISO
1911–1912	A. W. Gore
1912–1915	The Lord Desborough KCVO
1915–1921	H. Wilson Fox MP
1921–1929	H. W. W. Wilberforce
1929–1934	H.R.H. The Prince George KG
1934–1942	H.R.H. The Duke of Kent KG
1944–1961	H.R.H. The Duchess of Kent CI GCVO GBE
1961–1968	H.R.H. Princess Marina, Duchess of Kent CI GCVO GBE
1969–	H.R.H. The Duke of Kent KG GCMG GCVO ADC

Chairmen of the Club

Up to 1929 there was no permanently elected Chairman – the chair was normally taken at Committee meetings by the President.

1929–1936	Sir Herbert Wilberforce
1937–1953	Group Captain Sir Louis Greig KBE CVO DL
1953–1955	A. H. Riseley OBE
1955–1959	Dr. J. C. Gregory
1959–1974	H. F. David CBE
1974–1983	Air Chief Marshal Sir Brian Burnett GCB DFC AFC RAF (Ret'd.)
1983–1989	R. E. H. Hadingham CBE MC TD
1989–1999	J. A. H. Curry CBE
1999–2010	T. D. Phillips CBE
2010–	P. G. H. Brook

Secretaries/Chief Executives of the Club

In 1983 the Secretary became the Chief Executive.

1877–1879	J. H. Walsh	*1939–1945*	Miss N. G. Cleather (acting)
1880–1888	J. Marshall	*1946–1963*	Lt. Col. A. D. C. Macaulay OBE
1888–1891	H. W. W. Wilberforce	*1963–1979*	Major A. D. Mills
1891–1898	A. Chitty	*1979–2005*	C. J. Gorringe CBE
1899–1906	A. Palmer	*2005–2012*	I. R. Ritchie
1907–1925	Commander G. W. Hillyard	*2012–*	R.A. Lewis
1925–1939	Major D. T. R. Larcombe		

The Management of
The Championships

Committee of Management

The Championships are run by a Committee of Management consisting of the Committee of The All England Lawn Tennis Club (twelve members) and seven nominees of The Lawn Tennis Association, who form sub-committees with special responsibility for all major aspects of the meeting, e.g. commercial, catering, finance, ground, tennis and tickets.

Preparations

The preparations for The Championships start directly after the preceding meeting. Improvements are considered by the Committee of Management and the decisions taken are implemented from then onwards. Grass renovation to the Centre and No. 1 Courts starts immediately after The Championships and on the other courts during August and September.

Between Championships the Club has regular meetings with the London Borough of Merton, within which the Club is situated, and other interested parties to consider traffic and queuing problems experienced during the Fortnight and to monitor progress on remedies recommended.

Referee's Office

The Referee is the arbiter on any question involving interpretation of the rules of the game. He also runs the Qualifying Competition.

He and his four assistants are responsible for putting matches onto court, recording and displaying results, allocating the duties of umpires and line judges and undertaking a variety of other duties connected with the programme of matches.

Entries of Players

Players wishing to enter The Championships are required to submit their entry on a special form, which has to be submitted six weeks before The Championships begin. The Committee of Management, with the assistance of the Referee, use the computer ranking lists to determine which players are admitted directly into the Championship events, those who have to qualify and those who are rejected. The Committee use their discretion regarding the admission of "wild cards" in the draw.

About 500 entries, including juniors, are accepted. Of these 128 are included in the draw for the Gentlemen's and Ladies' Singles and 64 pairs for the Gentlemen's and Ladies' Doubles and 48 pairs for the Mixed Doubles .

The Qualifying Competition takes place in the week before The Championships at the Bank of England Sports Club, Roehampton.

Programme of Matches

The matches for each day are prepared in draft the previous evening by the Referee and submitted by him to the Order of Play committee for approval or amendment.

Every effort is made to have the potentially most attractive matches played on the courts with the most spectator accommodation but care has also to be taken to give any player likely to go far in the tournament his or her fair share of the show courts.

Junior Events

The International Tennis Federation's world computer ranking lists are used determine the entry of players into the Boys' and Girls' singles and doubles events. There are 64 singles players and 32 doubles pairs.

Invitation Doubles

The Ladies' Invitation Doubles, Gentlemens' Invitation Doubles and Gentlemens' Senior Invitation Doubles events are held during the second week of The Championships. The original invitation is extended to previous Champions, players of distinguished achievements at The Championships and active players on the senior circuit.

ATP World Tour Final

The Grand Slams, The International Tennis Federation and the ATP created a Gentlemen's season finale known as the Tennis Masters Cup in 2000. This jointly-owned event replaced both the Gentlemen's Grand Slam Cup and the ATP Tour World Championship. Starting in 2009 the season finale named the ATP World Tour Final and is held each year in London at the O2 Arena in November. The format of the event is an eight man singles round-robin, plus doubles , with prize money of more than $5 million. The best players in the annual ATP Champions Race, including Grand Slam Winners in the top 20, are eligible to compete.

Throughout their association with the Men's Year End event, the Grand Slams have continued to add to their remarkable and unique contribution to the international development of the sport. In the ten years of the Grand Slam Cup, the nine years of the Tennis Masters Cup and the first four years of the ATP World Tour Finals the Grand Slams have delivered more than $38 million to the Grand Slam Development Fund, which is administered by the ITF for the benefit of the game worldwide.

Competitors' Dress and Shoes

Since 1963 Wimbledon Championship Entry Conditions have laid down that except for a cardigan, pullover or headwear, competitors must be dressed predominantly in white throughout. In 1995 this condition was clarified to mean 'almost entirely in white'. Any competitor who appears on court dressed in a manner deemed unsuitable by the Committee will be liable to be defaulted.

No shoes, other than those with rubber soles, without heels, ribs, studs or coverings, shall be worn by competitors except with the express permission of the Referee.

Tie-Break

The tie-break scoring system, as authorised by the Rules, has been used since 1971, originally at 8-games all but since 1979 at 6-games all, other than in the final set.

Change of ends

Players will change ends (without sitting down) after the first game of each set, followed by a 90 seconds interval after each second game. At the end of each set, players will be allowed a two-minute break, regardless of the score in that set.

Chair Umpires and Line Umpires

There are 350 officials at The Championships working as Chair Umpires, Line Umpires or management staff. These officials cover over 650 matches played during the fortnight.

There are approximately 240 British officials, all members of the Association of British Tennis Officials (ABTO) and approximately 110 overseas officials from all over the world including the team of six ITF/Grand Slam Chair Umpires that officiates at all four Grand Slams, and two full time ATP officials.

Around 47 Chair Umpires are assigned each day, with the other officials working as Line Umpires. Chair Umpires normally umpire two matches a day, although not necessarily on the same court. Line Umpires work in teams, two teams being assigned to each court. The teams work on a timed rotation, 60 minutes on, 60 minutes off, with nine Line Umpires per team on Centre Court and Nos 1, 2 and 3 Courts and seven Line Umpires per team on other courts.

Chair Umpires use computers to score the match, each point scored being displayed automatically on the Club's website. Net cord machines are used by the Chair Umpire on all courts, and the Hawk-Eye electronic system is used on Centre, No. 1, No. 2 and No. 3 Courts to allow line calls to be reviewed. In order for the players, officials and spectators to see the line call being reviewed two 4.48m x 2.68m screens are sited at ground level on both Centre and No.1 Court.

LTA Officiating Department staff are responsible for all administrative arrangements of officials both before and during The Championships. They work closely with Jenny Higgs the Chief Umpire who is responsible for the overall management and assignment of Chair and Line Umpires during The Championships using a custom-made computer system and assisted by a small management team.

Chair and Line Umpires wear the Polo Ralph Lauren designed uniform introduced in 2006.

Ball Boys and Girls

In the twenties and thirties, the ball boys were provided by the Shaftesbury Homes. From 1946 they have been provided by volunteers from institutions and schools as follows: 1946 to 1966 - Dr Barnardo's Homes, 1967 to 1968, Shaftesbury Homes and since 1969 various schools in the London Borough of Merton and other adjacent Boroughs.

Training

Wimbledon training is directed by Sarah Goldson, currently teaching at Queen Mary's College, Basingstoke. The 2013 Championships will be Sarah's second year as manager following the retirement of Anne Rundle who was involved in Wimbledon training for over 35 years.

Training begins in February at the AELTC. Each prospective ball boy/girl will train once a fortnight and also attend four brief court training sessions at the Covered Courts before Easter. After the break all training takes place at Wimbledon (mainly on the Covered Courts) and lasts until mid June apart from school holidays.

Weekly training sessions last about two to two and a half hours with up to 60 children per session. Four sessions per week. Training sessions involve general fitness & movement exercises, circuits, ball skills (rolling, feeding, receiving, work on knowledge of the game), scoring (e.g.. knowing from the score at which end should the balls be), and set pieces (marching, start and end of game, tie break, ball change, suspended play etc.) Throughout training each candidate is constantly assessed on the above.

The Championships

During The Championships, four teams of six, selected by Sarah Goldson are responsible for the Centre and No. 1 Courts. Six teams of six rotate around the other show courts. The remainder in teams of six rotate around the other courts. The usual routine is one hour on and one hour off. The ball boys/girls usually arrive at 10.00 am and leave as soon as possible after the last court is closed.

The number of ball boys/girls has grown steadily over the years from the late thirties, when 46 were employed. In 1995 the figure noticeably increased from 138 to 182 to allow a full allocation of six to a court and in 2007 the number reached 250.

Ball girls were first introduced in 1977, and mixed teams in 1980. In 1986 ball girls were used on the Centre Court for the first time. In 1984 ball boys/girls were initially provided for the Qualifying Competition.

Crowd Management

The Association of Wimbledon Honorary Stewards is responsible for crowd management and acts as 'hosts' to the public, directing, advising and giving help and guidance to visitors. The members marshal the queues, inside and outside the grounds, and supervise the seating of spectators with the assistance of the volunteer Service Stewards, including military personnel on leave, and a contingent provided by the London Fire Brigade. Some 700 staff are engaged on the Club's behalf by G4S Security Services (U.K.) to control the entrance gates and provide security of the grounds.

Staff

An approximate list of officials and staff engaged for the duration of The Championships is as follows:–

Ball Boys and Girls 250	Groundsmen 20	Press staff 18
Ball distributors 7	Honorary Stewards 185	Referee's office 16
Buildings and Service Personnel 84	Housekeeping staff (day) 176	Security guards 700
Catering staff 1,800	Left Luggage office 30	Service stewards 595
Court attendants 180	Lift Operators 31	Speed of service operators 8
Court officials 310	Night Cleaners 163	Transport service drivers 320
Dressing room attendants 22	Physiotherapists 14	
Data Collectors 36	Practice Courts 8	

Tickets

Distribution

There has always been a considerable demand for tickets, especially since the advent of large-scale air travel and the consequent increase in the number of foreign visitors to Wimbledon and equitable distribution is inevitably a subject which causes much debate both within the Club and outside. However, only the Centre Court and No. 1 Court Debenture Holders, Members of the Club and Council Members of The Lawn Tennis Association obtain them as a matter of right.

Special allocations are made to British Tennis Membership and overseas Lawn Tennis Associations for distribution to their affiliated clubs, etc. and to other organisations with special claims. A set number of tickets for the Centre Court, No. 1 Court and No. 2 Court are allocated to schools affiliated to The Lawn Tennis Association.

A substantial proportion of the total number of tickets is retained for issue to the general public, either in advance, via annual public ballot, online on the day before play, or at the turnstiles on the day of play. The ballot for Centre Court, No. 1 Court, No. 2 Court tickets is held annually.

Centre Court and No. 1 Court

Sportsworld Group and Keith Prowse Hospitality have responsibility for selling U.K. and overseas packages for the Centre, No. 1 and No. 2 Courts. Sportsworld covers USA, Canada and Mexico and Keith Prowse Hospitality covers all territories in the world.

Daily Tickets and Admission

A limited number of tickets for reserved seats on the Centre Court are available for purchase at the ground each day, EXCEPT for the last four days. Also a limited number of tickets for No. 1 Court seats are available daily.

Tickets are available daily for No. 3 Court seats but only for as many days as a full programme of matches can be maintained.

Admission to the ground can be obtained only in Church Road, Gate 3, through the Museum Building, housing 20 turnstiles, via the queue in Wimbledon Park. Spectators are entitled to use the free standing enclosure on No. 3 Court and bench seating around other outside courts.

Wheelchair spaces and seats for The Lest We Forget and Not Forgotten Associations

As part of the current Centre Court development programme, the provision for wheelchair spectators was increased. There are now 20 spaces in the upper level, five spaces in the north east corner at courtside and three spaces at the southern end of the courts with 28 seats for guests. There are 40 spaces on the No. 1 Court together with seats for guests. On the No. 2 Court, 20 spaces and 20 seats for guests are available at the south end. On No. 3 Court 10 spaces are available. There are also unreserved areas for small number of wheelchairs by the side of all outside courts and a designated area on the Aorangi Terrace.

On Centre Court for the first 11 days and the No. 1 Court, for the first five days of each week 16 seats per day are allocated between the Lest We Forget and Not Forgotten Associations, whose members may include Chelsea Pensioners.

Re-sale of Used Tickets

Holders of tickets for reserved seats, who have to leave before the end of play, are requested to offer their tickets for scanning as they leave the grounds or to place their tickets in special red boxes from which they are collected. The tickets are then re-sold from a kiosk, situated north of No. 18 Court, near the top of St. Mary's Walk, for a nominal charge to other people in the grounds. This scheme started in 1954 and in total has raised over 1.5 million pounds. All monies are donated to charity. HSBC, the official banking partner of The Championships, has kindly agreed to donate to charity a sum equal to the total amount raised by the ticket sales each year since 2008.

The record amount collected was £167,000 at the 2012 Championships.

Times of Play

The whole grounds open at 10.30 a.m. daily. Play starts at 11.30 a.m. on Nos. 2–12, 14–19 Courts for at least the first eight days. Play starts at 1 p.m. on the Centre Court on the first 11 days and 2 p.m. on the two Finals days. Play starts on No. 1 Court at 1 p.m. each day. Junior matches start at 11 am from the first Saturday. In the event of rain, the Committee may need to alter these timings. Depending on the weather and length of matches, play normally finishes between 8 p.m. and 9 p.m.

Cancellation of Play due to Rain

Details of the Raincheck policy introduced in 2001 are as follows and apply to all 13 scheduled days of The Championships, including the final Sunday.

i. If there is less than one hour's play because of rain on the court for which tickets have been bought, the *original purchasers* of the tickets for that court on that day will be refunded with the amount which they paid for those tickets – the maximum refund payable will be the face value of the tickets for the day concerned.

ii. Purchasers of Grounds passes at the turnstiles (except those purchased after 5 p.m.) will be eligible for a full refund if, due to rain, the average amount of play on those courts accessible with a Grounds pass and for which play was originally scheduled is less than one hour.

iii. If there is more than one hour's play, but less than two hours' play, refunds will be limited to half the amount paid.

iv. The Referee's decision on how much play has taken place will be final.

v. Only the *original purchasers* are eligible for refunds under this policy. Refunds will be paid out automatically for tickets bought in advance, but tickets bought at the turnstiles (prior to 5 p.m. only) should be returned without delay to: The Ticket Office, 'Raincheck', PO Box 98, London SW19 5AE.

vi. In view of the numbers that could be involved, *please do not call the Ticket Office or telephone the AELTC.*

vii. Tickets purchased at the Ticket Resale kiosk are not covered by this policy as the monies are passed to charity.

viii. Separate terms and conditions apply (a) to Debenture Holders as notified by The All England Lawn Tennis Ground plc and (b) to any extra days of play.

Records at Wimbledon

Countries whose representatives have won the Gentlemen's Singles Championships (126)
Australia (21), Croatia (1), Czechoslovakia (1), Egypt (1), France (7), Germany (4), Great Britain (British Isles) (35), Netherlands (1), New Zealand (4), Serbia (1), Spain (3), Sweden (7), Switzerland (7) and the United States (33).

Countries whose representatives have won the Ladies' Singles Championships (119)
Australia (5), Brazil (3), Czech Republic (2), France (7), Germany (8), Great Britain (British Isles) (36), Russia (1), Spain (1), Switzerland (1) and the United States (55).

Winners of most Gentlemen's Singles Championships
7 W. C. Renshaw (G.B.) *1881–1886, 1889*
7 P. Sampras (U.S.A.) *1993–1995, 1997–2000*
7 R. Federer (Switzerland) *2003–2007, 2009, 2012*
5 H. L. Doherty (G.B.) *1902–1906*
5 B. R. Borg (Sweden) *1976–1980*
4 R. F. Doherty (G.B.) *1897–1900*
4 A. F. Wilding (N.Z.) *1910–1913*
4 R. G. Laver (Australia) *1961, 1962, 1968, 1969*
3 W. Baddeley (G.B.) *1891, 1892, 1895*
3 A. W. Gore (G.B.) *1901, 1908, 1909*
3 W. T. Tilden (U.S.A.) *1920, 1921, 1930*
3 F. J. Perry (G.B.) *1934–1936*
3 J. D. Newcombe (Australia) *1967, 1970, 1971*
3 J. P. McEnroe (U.S.A.) *1981, 1983, 1984*
3 B. F. Becker (Germany) *1985, 1986, 1989*

Winners of most Ladies' Singles Championships
9 Miss M. Navratilova (U.S.A.) *1978, 1979, 1982–1987, 1990*
8 Miss H. N. Wills/Mrs. F. S. Moody (U.S.A.) *1927–1930, 1932, 1933, 1935, 1938*
7 Miss D. K. Douglass/Mrs. R. L. Chambers (G.B.) *1903, 1904, 1906, 1910, 1911, 1913, 1914*
7 Miss S. M. Graf (Germany) *1988, 1989, 1991–1993, 1995, 1996*
6 Miss B. Bingley/Mrs. G. W. Hillyard (G.B.) *1886, 1889, 1894, 1897, 1899, 1900*
6 Miss S. R. F. Lenglen (France) *1919–1923, 1925*
6 Mrs. L. W. King (U.S.A.) *1966–1968, 1972, 1973, 1975*
5 Miss C. Dod (G.B.) *1887, 1888, 1891–1893*
5 Miss C. R. Cooper/Mrs. A. Sterry (G.B.) *1895, 1896, 1898, 1901, 1908*
5 Miss V. E. S. Williams (U.S.A.) *2000, 2001, 2005, 2007, 2008*
5 Miss S. J. Williams (U.S.A.) *2002, 2003, 2009, 2010, 2012*
4 Miss A. L. Brough (U.S.A.) *1948–1950, 1955*
3 Miss M. E. A. Bueno (Brazil) *1959, 1960, 1964*
3 Miss M. C. Connolly (U.S.A.) *1952–1954*
3 Miss M. Smith/Mrs. B. M. Court (Australia) *1963, 1965, 1970*
3 Miss C. M. Evert/Mrs J. M. Lloyd (U.S.A.) *1974, 1976, 1981*

Winners of most Gentlemen's Doubles Championships
9 T. A. Woodbridge (Australia) *1993–1997, 2000, 2002-2004*
8 H. L. Doherty (G.B.) *1897–1901, 1903–1905*
8 R. F. Doherty (G.B.) *1897–1901, 1903–1905*

Winner of most Ladies' Doubles Championships
12 Miss E. M. Ryan (U.S.A.) *1914, 1919–1923, 1925–1927, 1930, 1933, 1934*

Winners of Most Mixed Doubles Championships – Gentlemen
4 O. K. Davidson (Australia) *1967, 1971, 1973, 1974*
4 K. N. Fletcher (Australia) *1963, 1965, 1966, 1968*
4 E. V. Seixas (U.S.A.) *1953–1956*

Winner of most Mixed Doubles Championships – Ladies
7 Miss E. M. Ryan (U.S.A.) *1919, 1921, 1923, 1927, 1928, 1930, 1932*

Winner of most Singles, Doubles and Mixed Doubles Championships – Gentlemen
13 H. L. Doherty (G.B.) 5 singles, 8 doubles, *1897–1906*

Winner of most Singles, Doubles and Mixed Doubles Championships – Ladies
20 Miss B. J. Moffitt/Mrs. L. W. King (U.S.A.) 6 singles, 10 doubles, 4 mixed, *1961–1979*
20 Miss M. Navratilova (Czechoslovakia/USA), 9 singles, 7 doubles, 4 mixed *1976–2003*

Winners of Singles, Doubles and Mixed Doubles Championships in one year – Gentlemen
1937 J. D. Budge (U.S.A.)   *1939* R. L. Riggs (U.S.A.)
1938 J. D. Budge (U.S.A.)   *1952* F. A. Sedgman (Australia)

Winners of Singles, Doubles and Mixed Doubles Championships in one year – Ladies
1920 Miss S. R. F. Lenglen (France)   *1950* Miss A. L. Brough (U.S.A.)
1922 Miss S. R. F. Lenglen (France)   *1951* Miss D. J. Hart (U.S.A.)
1925 Miss S. R. F. Lenglen (France)   *1967* Mrs. L. W. King (U.S.A.)
1939 Miss A. Marble (U.S.A.)   *1973* Mrs. L. W. King (U.S.A.)
1948 Miss A. L. Brough (U.S.A.)

The Youngest Champions
Gentlemen's Singles – B. F. Becker (Germany) 17 years, 227 days *1985*
Ladies' Singles   – Miss C. Dod (G.B.) 15 years, 285 days *1887*
Gentlemen's Doubles – R. D. Ralston (U.S.A.) 17 years, 341 days *1960*
Ladies' Doubles   – Miss M. Hingis (Switzerland) 15 years, 282 days *1996*
Mixed Doubles   – R. G. Laver (Australia) 20 years, 328 days *1959*
                     – Miss S.J. Williams (U.S.A.) 16 years, 282 days *1998*

The Oldest Champions
Gentlemen's Singles – A. W. Gore (G.B.) 41 years, 182 days *1909*
Ladies' Singles   – Mrs. A Sterry (G.B.) 37 years, 282 days *1908*
Gentlemen's Doubles – G. P. Mulloy (U.S.A.) 43 years, 226 days *1957*
Ladies' Doubles   – Miss E. M. Ryan (U.S.A.) 42 years, 152 days *1934*
Mixed Doubles   – S. E. Stewart (U.S.A.) 42 years, 28 days 1988
                     – Miss M. Navratilova (USA), 46 years 261 days (2003)

The Youngest Competitors
Gentlemen's Singles – S. B. B. Wood (U.S.A.) 15 years, 231 days *1927*
Ladies' Singles   – Miss J. M. Capriati (U.S.A.) 14 years, 90 days *1990*
                     – Miss K. Rinaldi (U.S.A.) 14 years, 91 days *1981*

The Oldest Competitors
Gentlemen's Singles – M. J. G. Ritchie (GB) 55 years, 247 days *1926*
Ladies' Singles   – Mrs. A. E. O'Neill (G.B.) 54 years, 304 days *1922*

The Youngest Seeds
Gentlemen's Singles – B. R. Borg (Sweden) 17 years, 19 days *1973*
Ladies' Singles   – Miss J. M. Capriati (U.S.A.) 14 years, 89 days *1990*

The Oldest Seeds
Gentlemen's Singles   –   R. A. Gonzales (U.S.A.) 41 years, 45 days *1969*
Ladies' Singles   –   Mrs. L. W. King (U.S.A.) 39 years, 210 days *1983*

Left-Handed Champions – Gentlemen

N. E. Brookes	(Australia)	S 1907, 1914, D 1907, 1914
J. B. Gilbert	(G.B.)	M 1924
J. Drobny	(Egypt)	S 1954
M. G. Rose	(Australia)	D 1954, M 1957
N. A. Fraser	(Australia)	S 1960, D 1959, 1961, M 1962
R. G. Laver	(Australia)	S 1961, 1962, 1968, 1969 D 1971, M 1959, 1960
A. D. Roche	(Australia)	D 1965, 1968–1970, 1974, M 1976
O. K. Davidson	(Australia)	M 1967, 1971, 1973, 1974
J. S. Connors	(U.S.A.)	S 1974, 1982, D 1973
J. P. McEnroe	(U.S.A.)	S 1981, 1983, 1984 D 1979, 1981, 1983, 1984, 1992
R. D. Leach	(U.S.A.)	D 1990, M 1990
M. R. Woodforde	(Australia)	D 1993–1997, 2000 M 1993
D. J. Johnson	(U.S.A.)	D 2001 M 2000
G. S. Ivanisevic	(Croatia)	S 2001
R. C. Bryan	(U.S.A)	D 2006, 2011, M2008
M. Llodra	(France)	D 2007
R. Nadal	(Spain)	S 2008, 2010
D. M. Nestor	(Canada)	D 2008, 2009
J. Melzer	(Austria)	D 2010

Left-Handed Champions – Ladies

Mrs L. A. Harper	(U.S.A.)	M 1931
Miss K. E. Stammers	(G.B.)	D 1935, 1936
Mrs. P. F. Jones	(G.B.)	S 1969, M 1969
Miss M. Navratilova	(U.S.A.)	S 1978, 1979, 1982–1987, 1990 D 1976, 1979, 1981–1984, 1986, M 1985, 1993, 1995, 2003.
Miss P. Kvitova	(CZE)	S 2011
Miss I. Benesova	(CZE)	M 2011

Double-Handed Champions – Gentlemen

J. E. Bromwich (FH)	(Australia)	D 1948, 1950, M 1947, 1948
R. N. Howe (BH)	(Australia)	M 1958
F. D. McMillan (FH & BH)	(SA)	D 1967, 1972, 1978, M 1978, 1981
J. S. Connors (BH)	(U.S.A.)	S 1974, 1982, D 1973
B. R. Borg (BH)	(Sweden)	S 1976–1980
P. F. McNamee (BH)	(Australia)	D 1980, 1982, M 1985
K. J. Nystrom (BH)	(Sweden)	D 1986
M. A. O. Wilander (BH)	(Sweden)	D 1986
K. E. Flach (BH)	(U.S.A.)	D 1987, 1988, M 1986
A. P. Jarryd (BH)	(Sweden)	D 1989, 1991
R. D. Leach	(U.S.A.)	D 1990, M 1990
J. R. Pugh (FH & BH)	(U.S.A.)	D 1990, M 1989
A. K. Agassi (BH)	(U.S.A.)	S 1992
M. R. Woodforde (BH)	(Australia)	D 1993–1997, 2000 M 1993
J. A. Stark (BH)	(U.S.A.)	M 1995
P. V. N. Haarhuis (BH)	(Netherlands)	D 1998

The 2012 Singles Champions – Roger Federer (Switzerland) and Serena Williams (U.S.A)

M. S. Bhupathi (BH)	(India)	D 1999, M2002, 2003
G. Ivanisevic (BH)	(Croatia)	S 2001
L. G. Hewitt (BH)	(Australia)	S 2002
J. L. Bjorkman (BH)	(Sweden)	D 2002-2004
W. H. Black (BH)	(Zimbabwe)	M 2004
A. Clement (BH)	(France)	D 2007
R. Nadal (BH)	(Spain)	S 2008
D. M. Nestor (BH)	(Canada)	D 2008, 2009
J. Melzer (BH)	(Austria)	D 2010
P. Petzschner (BH)	(Germany)	D 2010
N. Djokovic	(Serbia)	S 2011
F.L Nielsen	(Denmark)	D2012

Double-Handed Champions – Ladies

Miss C. M. Evert/		
Mrs. J. M. Lloyd (BH)	(U.S.A.)	S 1974, 1976, 1981, D 1976
Miss T. A. Austin (BH)	(U.S.A.)	M 1980
Miss N. M. Zvereva (BH)	(U.R.S./C.I.S/ B.L.S.)	D 1991–1994, 1997
Miss A. I. M. Sanchez Vicario (BH)	(Spain)	D 1995
Miss M. Hingis (BH)	(Switzerland)	S 1997, D 1996, 1998
Miss S. J. Williams (BH)	(U.S.A.)	S 2002, 2003, 2009, 2010, 2012 D 2000, 2002, 2008, 2009, 2012, M 1998
Miss L. A. Davenport (BH)	(U.S.A.)	S 1999, D 1999
Miss V. E. S. Williams (BH)	(U.S.A.)	S 2000, 2001, 2005, 2007, 2008, D 2000, 2002, 2008, 2009, 2012
Miss K. Y. Po (BH)	(U.S.A.)	M 2000
Miss D. Hantuchova (BH)	(Slovak Rep.)	M 2001
Miss E. Likhovtseva (BH)	(Russia)	M 2002
Miss K. Clijsters (BH)	(Belgium)	D 2003
Miss A. Sugiyama (BH)	(Japan)	D 2003
Miss C. C. Black (BH)	(Zimbabwe)	D 2004, 2005, 2007, M 2004
Miss M. Sharapova (BH)	(Russia)	S 2004
Mrs A. Huber (BH)	(S.A.)	D 2005, 2007
Miss M. C. Pierce (BH)	(France)	M 2005
Miss Z. Yan (BH)	(China)	D 2006
Miss J. Zheng (BH)	(China)	D 2006
Miss V. Zvonareva (BH)	(Russia)	M 2006
Miss J. Jankovic (BH)	(Serbia)	M 2007
Miss S. J. Stosur (BH)	(Australia)	M 2008
Miss A-L. Groenefeld	(Germany)	M 2009
Miss V. King (BH)	(U.S.A.)	D 2010
Miss Y. V. Shvedova (BH)	(Kazakhstan)	D 2010
Miss P. Kvitova	(Czech Rep.)	S 2011
Miss K. Srebotnik	(Slovakia)	D 2011
Miss I. Benesova	(Czech Rep.)	M 2011
Mrs T. Peschke	(Czech Rep.)	D 2011

Unseeded Gentlemen's Singles Champions

Since full seeding began in 1927 only two unseeded players have won the title: B.F. Becker (Germany) in 1985 and G.S. Ivanisevic (Croatia) in 2001.

An unseeded player has reached the final 12 times:

W. L. Allison (U.S.A.) *1930*   W. P. Bungert (Germany) *1967*

K. Neilsen (Denmark) *1953*
K. Neilsen (Denmark) *1955*
R. G. Laver (Australia) *1959*
M. F. Mulligan (Australia) *1962*
F. S. Stolle (Australia) *1963*
C. J. Lewis (N.Z.) *1983*
B. F. Becker (Germany) *1985*
M. O. Washington (U.S.A.) *1996*
C. A. Pioline (FRA) *1997*
G. S. Ivanisevic (CRO) *2001*

Unseeded Ladies' Singles Champions

Since full seeding began in 1927 an unseeded player has never won the title. The lowest seed to win the title was Miss. V. E. S. Williams (U.S.A) at No.23 in 2007.

An unseeded player has reached the final four times:

Miss H. H. Jacobs (U.S.A.) *1938*   Mrs. V. Sukova (Czechoslovakia) *1962*
Miss F. A. M. Mortimer (G.B.) *1958* Miss B. J. Moffitt (U.S.A.) *1963*

Most Games in a Match

Gentlemen's Singles – 183 J. R. Isner (U.S.A.) bt N. Mahut (FRA) 6-4 3-6 6-7 (7-9) 7-6(7-3) 70-68 *2010, First Round* (11hrs 5mins)

Ladies' Singles – 58 Miss C.R. Rubin (U.S.A.) bt Mrs P. Hy-Boulais (CAN) 7-6 (7-4) 6-7 (5-7) 17-15 *1995, Second Round*

Gentlemen's Doubles – 102 M.P.D. Melo and A.R. Sa (BRA) bt P.J. Handley (AUS) and K.R. Ullyett (ZIM) 5-7 7-6(7-4) 4-6 7-6(9-7) 28-26 (*2007 - Second Round*)

Ladies' Doubles – 50 Miss M. Hingis (Switzerland) and Miss A.I.M. Sanchez Vicario (Spain) bt Miss C.R. Rubin (U.S.A.) and Mrs. S. Schultz McCarthy (Netherlands) 7-6 (14-12) 6-7 (6-8) 13-11 *1997 Third Round*

Mixed Doubles – 77 M. Schapers and Miss B. Schultz (Netherlands) bt T. Nijssen (Netherlands) and Miss A. Temesvari (Hungary) 6-3 5-7 29-27 *1991, First Round*

Most Games in a Set

– 138 J. R. Isner (U.S.A.) bt N. Mahut (FRA) 6-4 3-6 6-7(7-9) 7-6(7-3) 70-68 *2010, First Round*

– 46 R. A. Gonzales (U.S.A.) bt C.M. Pasarell (U.S.A.) 22-24 1-6 16-14 6-3 11-9 *1969, First Round*

Ladies' Singles – 32 Miss C.R. Rubin (U.S.A.) bt Mrs P. Hy-Boulais (CAN) 7-6 (7-4) 6-7 (5-7) 17-15 *1995, Second Round*

Gentlemen's Doubles – 62 A.R. Olmedo (Peru) and P. Segura (Ecuador) bt G. L. Forbes (S.A.) and A. A. Segal (S.A.) 32-30 5-7 6-4 6-4 *1968, Second Round*

Ladies' Doubles – 32 Miss L. Horn (RSA) and Miss K. Srebotnik (SLO) bt Miss K. Boogert (NED) and Miss A-G. Sidot (FRA) 6-4 1-6 17-15 *1999, Quarter Final*

Mixed Doubles – 56 M. Schapers and Miss B. Schultz (Netherlands) bt T. Nijssen (Netherlands) and Miss A. Temesvari (Hungary) 6-3 5-7 29-27 *1991, First Round*

Most Games in a Final

Gentlemen's Singles – 77 R. Federer (Switzerland) bt A. S. Roddick (USA) 5-7 7-6 (8-6) 7-6 (7-5) 3-6 16-14 *2009*

Ladies' Singles – 46 Mrs. B. M. Court (Australia) bt Mrs. L. W. King (U.S.A.) 14-12 11-9 *1970 Note:* In 1902 Miss M.E. Robb (G.B.) bt Mrs. A Sterry (G.B.) 7-5 6-1 after abandoning the match started the day before, due to rain, with the score at 4-6 13-11. The total games played were 53.

Gentlemen's Doubles – 83 J. P. McEnroe (U.S.A.) and M. D. Stich (Germany) bt J. F. Grabb and R. A. Reneberg (U.S.A.) 5-7 7-6 3-6 7-6 19-17 *1992*

Ladies' Doubles – 38 Mrs R. Mathieu (France) and Miss E.M. Ryan (U.S.A.) bt Miss W. A. James (G.B.) and Miss A. M. Yorke (G.B.) 6-2 9-11 6-4 *1933*

– 38 Miss R. Casals (U.S.A.) and Mrs. L. W. King (U.S.A.) bt Miss M. E.A. Bueno (Brazil) and Miss N. A. Richey (U.S.A.) 9-11 6-4 6-2 *1967*

– 38 Miss S. M. Graf (Germany) and Miss G. B. Sabatini (Arg) bt Miss L. Savchenko and Miss N. M. Zvereva (U.S.S.R.) 6-3 1-6 12-10 *1988*

Mixed Doubles – 48 E. W. Sturgess (S.A.) and Mrs. R. A. Summers (S.A.) bt J. E. Bromwich (Australia) and Miss A. L. Brough (U.S.A.) 9-7 9-11 7-5 *1949*

Least Games in a Final

Gentlemen's Singles – 20 W. C. Renshaw (G.B.) bt J. T. Hartley (G.B.) 6-0 6-1 6-1 (37 minutes) *1881*

– 20 F. J. Perry (G.B.) bt G. Von Cramm (Germany) 6-1 6-1 6-0 (40 minutes) *1936*

Ladies' Singles – 12 Mrs. R. L. Chambers (G.B.) bt Miss P. D. H. Boothby (G.B.) 6-0 6-0 (24 minutes) *1911*

Gentlemen's Doubles – 22 M. J. G. Ritchie (G.B.) and A. F. Wilding (N.Z.) bt A. W. Gore (G.B.) and H. R. Barrett (G.B.) 6-1 6-1 6-2 *1910*

Ladies' Doubles – 12 Miss S. J. Fry (U.S.A.) and Miss D. J. Hart (U.S.A.) bt Miss M. C. Connolly (U.S.A.) and Miss J. A. Sampson (U.S.A.) 6-0 6-0 *1953*

Mixed Doubles – 12 R. Lycett (G.B.) and Miss E. M. Ryan (U.S.A.) bt A. D. Prebble (G.B.) and Mrs R. L. Chambers (G.B.) 6-0 6-0 *1919*

Longest Finals

Gentlemen's Singles – 4 hours 48 mins R. Nadal (Spain) bt R. Federer (Switzerland) 6-4 6-4 6-7 (5-7) 6-7 (8-10) 9-7 *2008*

Ladies' Singles – 2 hours 46 mins. Miss V. E. S. Williams (U.S.A.) bt Miss L. A. Davenport (Mrs J. Leach) 4-6 7-6 (7-4) 9-7 *2005*

Shortest Finals

Gentlemen's Singles – 37 mins. W. C. Renshaw (G.B.) bt J. T. Hartley (G.B.) 6-0 6-1 6-1 *1881*

– 40 mins. F. J. Perry (G.B.) bt G. Von Cramm (Germany) 6-1 6-1 6-0 *1936*

Ladies' Singles – 23 mins. Miss S.R.F. Lenglen (France) bt Mrs. F. I. Mallory (U.S.A.) 6-2 6-0 *1922*

– 24 mins. Mrs. R. L. Chambers (G.B.) bt Miss P. D. H. Boothby (G.B.) 6-0 6-0 *1911*

Most Points in a Tie-break

Gentlemen's Singles – 38 B. R. Borg (Sweden) bt P. J. Lall (India) 6-3 6-4 9-8 (20-18) *1973, First Round*

Ladies' Singles – 28 Miss S. V. Wade (G.B.) bt Miss J. M. Durie (G.B.) 3-6 7-6 (15-13) 6-2 *1982, First Round*

Gentlemen's Doubles – 50 J. Gunnarson (Sweden) and M. Mortensen (Denmark) bt J. Frawley (Australia) and V. Pecci (Paraguay) 6-3 6-4 3-6 7-6 (26-24) *1985, First Round*

Ladies Doubles – 26 Miss M. Hingis (Switzerland) and Miss A.I.M. Sanchez Vicario (Spain) bt Miss C.R. Rubin (U.S.A.) and Mrs. S. Schultz McCarthy (Netherlands) 7-6 (14-12) 6-7 (6-8) 13-11 *1997, Third Round*

Gentlemen's Singles Final – 34 B. R. Borg (Sweden) bt J. P. McEnroe (U.S.A.) 1-6 7-5 6-3 6-7 (16-18) 8-6 *1980*

Ladies' Singles Final – 14 Miss S. M. Graf (Germany) bt Miss J. Novotna (Czech Republic) 7-6 (8-6) 1-6 6-4 *1993*

Gentlemen's Doubles Final – 26 D.M. Nestor (CAN) and N. Zimonjic (SRB) bt J.L. Bjorkman and K.R. Ullyett (ZIM) 7-6 (14-12) 6-7 (3-7) 6-3 6-3 *(2008)*

Ladies' Doubles Final – 18 Mrs. G. E. Reid and Miss W. M. Turnbull (Australia) bt Miss M. Jausovec (Yugoslavia) and Miss V. Ruzici (Romania) 4-6 9-8 (10-8) 6-3 *1978*

Mixed Doubles Final – 22 M. J. Bates and Miss J. M. Durie (G.B.) bt D. J. Cahill and Miss N. A-L. Provis (Australia) 7-6 (12-10) 6-3 *1987*

Index

Printed by Remous Ltd., Milborne Port, Dorset.